HOCKEY SUPERSTARS

1998 ★ 1999

Paul Romanuk

Sixteen Super Mini-Posters of Top Hockey Stars
with Quotes and Facts and Useful Information
plus Your Own Record Keeper

FIREFLY BOOKS

A FIREFLY BOOK

Published in 1998 in the United States by:

Firefly Books (U.S.) Inc.
P.O. Box 1338
Ellicott Station
Buffalo, New York
14205

Original text © 1998 by Scholastic Canada Ltd.
Published by arrangement with Scholastic Canada Ltd.

Cataloguing in Publication Data
The National Library of Canada has catalogued this publication as follows:

Romanuk, Paul
   Hockey superstars

Annual.
Description based on: 1994/1995.
Published by Firefly Books, 1996-
ISSN 1201-8872
ISBN 1-55209-269-0 (1998-1999)

1. Hockey players—Biography—Periodicals.
2. National Hockey League—Biography—Periodicals.
I. Title.

GV848.5.A1R65   796.962   C98-300083-2

Photo Credits

Dominik Hasek (cover), John LeClair © 1998 J. McIsaac, Bruce Bennett Studios;
Wayne Gretzky © 1998 J. Leary, Bruce Bennett Studios;
Peter Forsberg, Mattias Ohlund © 1998 A. Foxall, Bruce Bennett Studios;
Martin Brodeur © 1998 Rick Berk, Bruce Bennett Studios;
Nicklas Lidstrom, Jaromir Jagr, Alexi Yashin © 1998 A Pichette, Bruce Bennett Studios;
Patrick Roy, Mats Sundin © 1998 C. Andersen, Bruce Bennett Studios;
Shayne Corson © 1998 J. Giamundo, Bruce Bennett Studios;
Eric Lindros © 1998 G. James, Protography;
Theoren Fleury © 1998 Bruce Bennett Studios;
Paul Kariya © 1998 H. DiRocco, Bruce Bennett Studios;
Mike Modano © 1998 Protography;
Keith Tkachuk © 1998 Bruce Bennett, Bruce Bennett Studios;
Paul Romanuk (back cover) © 1997, Kari Kerr

Printed and bound in Canada

★ ★ ★ **YOUR RECORD KEEPER** ★ ★ ★

Your Favorite Team — fill this part in at the beginning of the season.

Name of your favorite team: _____

Conference: _____

Division: _____

Players on your favorite team at the start of the season

Number	Name	Position
____	_____	_____
____	_____	_____
____	_____	_____
____	_____	_____
____	_____	_____
____	_____	_____
____	_____	_____
____	_____	_____
____	_____	_____
____	_____	_____
____	_____	_____
____	_____	_____
____	_____	_____
____	_____	_____
____	_____	_____
____	_____	_____
____	_____	_____
____	_____	_____
____	_____	_____

Changes, Trades, New Players

Fill this section in any time during the season. Use this space to write the names of players who join your team after the start of the season:

_____

_____

_____

_____

I. The Team Standings

Circle the team you think will finish in first place in each of the four NHL Divisions.

WESTERN CONFERENCE

Pacific Division	**Central Division**	**Northwest Division**
Anaheim Mighty Ducks	Chicago Blackhawks	Calgary Flames
Dallas Stars	Detroit Red Wings	Colorado Avalanche
Los Angeles Kings	Nashville Predators	Edmonton Oilers
Phoenix Coyotes	St. Louis Blues	Vancouver Canucks
San Jose Sharks		

EASTERN CONFERENCE

Atlantic Division	**Northeast Division**	**Southeast Division**
Pittsburgh Penguins	Toronto Maple Leafs	Carolina Hurricanes
New Jersey Devils	Boston Bruins	Florida Panthers
New York Islanders	Buffalo Sabres	Tampa Bay Lightning
New York Rangers	Montreal Canadiens	Washington Capitals
Philadelphia Flyers	Ottawa Senators	

II. The Playoffs

Which two teams will meet in the Stanley Cup Final?

Western Conference Winner: Eastern Conference Winner:

_____   _____

III. Stanley Cup Final

Which team will win the Stanley Cup?

_____

Your Team — All Season Long

You can keep track of your team's record all season.

The standings of hockey teams are listed on the sports page of the newspaper all season long. The standings will show you which team is in first place, second place, etc., right down to last place.

Some of the abbreviations you will become familiar with are: GP for games played; W for wins; L for losses; T for ties; PTS for points; A for assists; G for goals.

Check the standings on the same day of every month and copy down what they say about your team. By keeping track of your team in this manner you will be able to see when it was playing well and when it wasn't.

Your team: _____ month by month

(Put the name of your team here.)

DATE	GP	W	L	T	PTS
OCTOBER 1					
NOVEMBER 1					
DECEMBER 1					
JANUARY 1					
FEBRUARY 1					
MARCH 1					
APRIL 1					

Final Standings

At the end of the season print the final record of your team below.

Your Team	GP	W	L	T	PTS

Your Favorite Players' Scoring Records

While you're keeping track of your favorite team during the season, you can also follow the progress of your favorite players. Just fill in their point totals at the start of each month. The abbreviation for points is PTS.

PLAYER	OCT 1	NOV 1	DEC 1	JAN 1	FEB 1	MAR 1	APR 1

Your Favorite Goaltenders' Records

You can keep track of your favorite goaltenders' averages during the season. Just fill in the information below.

GAA is the abbreviation for Goals-Against Average. That is the average number of goals given up by a goaltender during a game over the course of the season.

PLAYER	OCT 1	NOV 1	DEC 1	JAN 1	FEB 1	MAR 1	APR 1

Tape the list here. How many of your picks are on the team?

At the end of the season you can get the final statistics for your favorite players and the rest of the league.

Fill in the leading scorer and the leading goaltender after the season is over.

NHL Leading Scorer	GP	G	A	PTS

NHL Leading Goaltender	GP	W	L	T	SO	GAA

Your All-Star Picks

Every year at the end of the hockey season, the Professional Hockey Writers Association selects the NHL's First and Second All-Star Teams. Here's a chance for you to make your selections. Remember to pick a player for every position.

First Team

Goaltender:_____

Left Defence:_____

Right Defence:_____

Center:_____

Left Wing:_____

Right Wing:_____

Second Team

Goaltender:_____

Left Defence:_____

Right Defence:_____

Center:_____

Left Wing:_____

Right Wing:_____

The list of the winners will be printed in the newspaper at the end of the season. Tape the list here. How many of your picks are on the team?

MARTIN BRODEUR
New Jersey Devils

It's hard to believe now, but when Martin Brodeur headed off to the New Jersey Devils training camp in September of 1993, he wasn't quite sure if he would make the team.

"I remember I had a new paint job on my mask," recalls Martin. "I had the flames on the side of it and the Devils logo on the front. But I only had the Devil, I didn't put the *N* part of the logo on because I wasn't sure that I would be in New Jersey. I didn't want to be in the minors with New Jersey on my mask. It wouldn't have looked very good."

Martin was playing it safe, but as it turned out, he didn't really have anything to worry about. He ended up playing 47 games in his rookie season with the Devils and was voted rookie of the year.

Martin has continued to excel. In only five NHL seasons he has won over 150 games. So far in his career he has recorded 32 shut-outs, including 10 last season. In each of the last two seasons he has finished with a goals-against average below 2.00!

"It just gives you so much confidence to play in front of him," says teammate Scott Niedermayer. "When a team has a good goalie playing, it makes you more confident in the things you can do as a player because you know he's going to be there with the save when you need it."

There are high expectations placed on every player in the NHL and to keep your job you have to work hard. But the pressures placed on a goaltender are even a little higher than those placed on most players. After all, every time the goalie makes a mistake, the red light goes on. It's not the same for a defenceman or a forward.

"It's really different playing goal," says Martin. "You have to be a bit of a loner. Hockey is a team game but goal is a position that you play by yourself. You need a lot of confidence."

Marty McSorley, a 15-season veteran of the NHL, says that the question you ask yourself when deciding whether or not a goalie can do the job for your team is: Could he play in the seventh game of the Stanley Cup Final?

"If the answer to that question isn't yes," says Marty, "then you don't have your guy. He has to have the confidence to face that kind of pressure . . . he has to want that kind of pressure. His teammates can feel that."

When it comes to Martin Brodeur, the New Jersey Devils can be confident that they have their man.

STATS
Martin Brodeur

- New Jersey's 1st pick (20th overall) 1990 NHL Entry Draft
- First NHL Team & Season — New Jersey Devils 1993–94
- Born — May 6, 1972, in Montreal, Quebec
- Position — Goaltender
- Catches — Left
- Height — 1.85 m (6'1")
- Weight — 92.3 kg (205 lbs.)

MARTIN BRODEUR

Goaltender
NEW JERSEY DEVILS

SHAYNE CORSON
Montreal Canadiens

Shayne Corson had a lot to prove heading into last season. At the age of 31, he was heading into the final stage of his NHL career. Could Shayne still make a meaningful contribution to his team, or should he be thinking about retiring? Shayne answered his critics by coming to training camp in the best shape of his career.

"I wanted to prove to people that, at 31, I was still young and in shape and a good NHL player," said Shayne.

Shayne worked with a personal trainer in the off-season and the benefits showed up in his on-ice performance. He impressed his coach enough to earn a spot on the team's top line with Saku Koivu and Mark Recchi.

"When Shayne is working hard and doing his job he brings a lot to our team," says coach Alain Vigneault. "We were all impressed with the shape that Shayne showed up in at camp and in all of the hard work that he put in during the summer."

Shayne started the season at a great pace with 32 points in the first two months. His solid play was enough to earn him a berth on Canada's Olympic team.

"I thought about making that team during the summer while I was training," recalls Shayne. "I had played in a couple of World Championships and in the 1991 Canada Cup. The Canada Cup was one of the greatest experiences I've ever had. So using the Olympic team as motivation was good for me."

Shayne finished up last season with 21 goals and 55 points. He missed a total of 20 games with a couple of nagging injuries.

Still, 55 points was his best single season total since 1993–94 when he was with the Edmonton Oilers. Shayne started his career with Montreal back in 1986–87 but was traded to Edmonton, spending three seasons with the Oilers and then a season and a half with St. Louis before returning to the team that gave him his start.

"I've always liked playing in Montreal," says Shayne. "It's a great hockey city and the fans and the management expect a lot out of you. But that just makes you better."

That ethic of hard work and high expectations has seen the Canadiens win more Stanley Cup championships than any other franchise in the NHL — 23 in total. And on all of those teams, they've needed a dedicated, hard-working veteran player like Shayne Corson. They're hoping he can help them to Cup number 24.

STATS
Shayne Corson

- Montreal's 2nd choice (8th overall) 1984 NHL Entry Draft
- First NHL Team & Season — Montreal Canadiens 1986–87
- Born — August 13, 1966, in Midland, Ontario
- Position — Left wing
- Shoots — Left
- Height — 1.85 m (6'1")
- Weight — 90 kg (200 lbs.)

SHAYNE CORSON

Left Wing
MONTREAL CANADIENS

THEOREN FLEURY
Calgary Flames

If you want to get Theoren Fleury talking, maybe even get him a little emotional, just ask him about his many experiences representing Canada in international hockey. There is no one who feels more for the flag he wears than Theoren.

"I owe where I am now to being able to play for Canada and have people notice me," says Theo. "Under-17 tournaments, under-18 and the World Junior Championships . . . that's where I had people notice how I could compete."

The way Theoren competes is with intensity and heart. Theoren is smaller than most NHL players, but his drive and desire to win more than make up for his lack of size. That is not to say that Theo doesn't have his fair share of skill. He could not have racked up the kind of offensive totals that he has with hard work alone. In 10 NHL seasons, Theoren has scored over 300 goals and more than 700 points.

"I think people overlook Fleury's skill sometimes," says his coach Brian Sutter. "Theo's one of the hardest working players in the game but he's also an excellent playmaker. That takes a lot of skill."

That combination of hard work and skill helped the Calgary Flames win a Stanley Cup Championship in 1989, Theo's rookie season. However, as rewarding as his NHL career has been, many of Theo's fondest hockey memories have come while he was wearing a Team Canada uniform.

"Each time you get to play for Canada it is something special. I have some great memories of each and every experience," says Theoren.

Aside from his Olympic appearance last season, Theo was also the captain of the Canadian team that won the World Junior Hockey Championship in 1988. In 1991, he played for Canada at the World Hockey Championship (winning silver) and on the Canada Cup-winning team. He also played on the Canadian team in the 1996 World Cup, where Canada finished second. There will undoubtedly be more international appearances before his career is finished.

"I've always had a passion for the game," says Theo. "The game and the way we play it in Canada has given me so much, coming from where I came from and the obstacles I've had to overcome. We play the game the way it should be played, with our hearts. We'll go that extra mile to do whatever it takes to win."

STATS
Theoren Fleury

- Calgary's 9th pick (166th overall) 1987 NHL Entry Draft
- First NHL Team & Season — Calgary Flames 1988–89
- Born — June 29, 1968, in Oxbow, Saskatchewan
- Position — Right wing
- Shoots — Right
- Height — 1.66 m (5'6')
- Weight — 72 kg (160 lbs.)

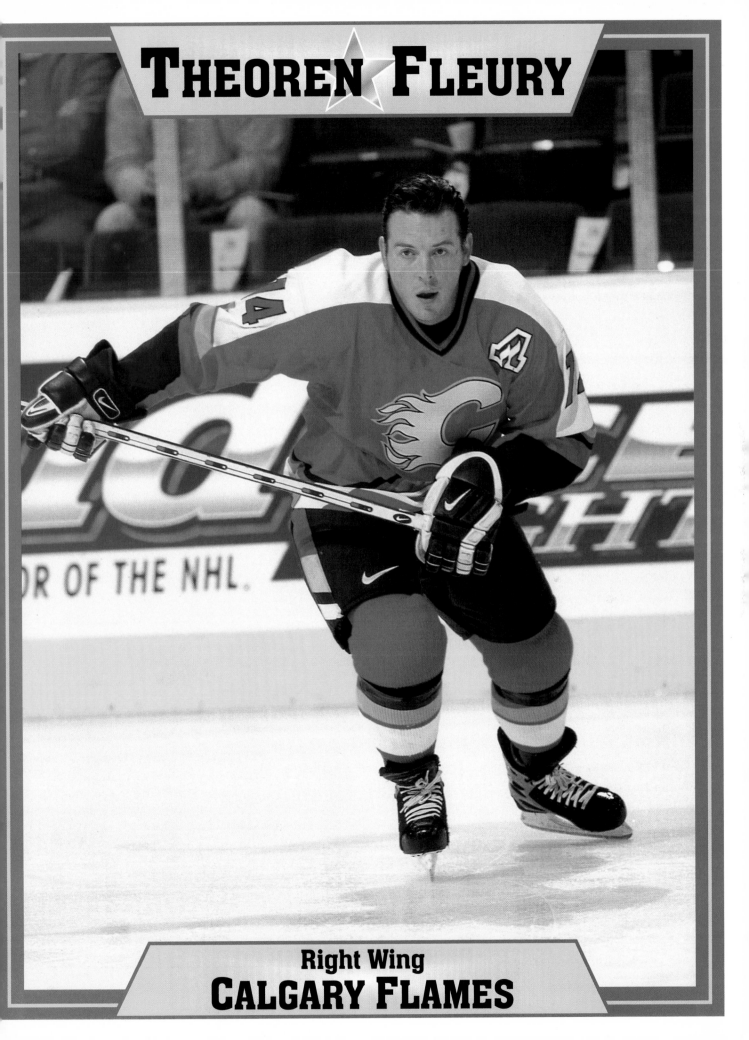

PETER FORSBERG
Colorado Avalanche

Peter Forsberg can score goals and rack up assists — there has never been any doubt about that. But the aspect of his game that earns him so much respect from opponents is his fiery competitive streak — Peter never backs down when it comes to hockey.

What Peter does back down from, however, is self-praise. A man who has averaged more than 25 goals per season in his four-year NHL career doesn't think he has a very good shot! That is not an opinion that his coach, Marc Crawford, shares.

"Peter is wrong about his shot," says the coach. "He has a very good shot. It's accurate. He just has to use it more if he wants to become the great scorer we all know he can be."

Peter is reluctant to talk about his defensive ability. The way he plays, he could easily win the NHL scoring title and the Selke Trophy as the league's top defensive forward in the same season. Teammate Joe Sakic says that Peter is "probably the most complete player in the game." But don't try to convince Peter that he is a defensive player.

"I don't really want to be the most defensive forward," says Peter. "I don't think that I play that type of game. I help out in my own end. I think that is an important part of the game, but I'm mostly an offensive player."

Any shy characteristics displayed by Peter off the ice during interviews are nowhere to be found once he steps onto the ice and into a game situation.

"He's a fierce competitor," says Chicago defenceman Chris Chelios, a noted tough competitor himself. Peter's combination of toughness and offensive skill makes him one of the best two-way players in the game. Another aspect of his game that draws attention is his determination to succeed.

"Peter has the great ability of being able to focus himself on the task at hand," says his coach Marc Crawford. "Other teams try to get him off his game by running at him and trying to intimidate him but it just doesn't work. He just becomes more focused."

For a guy who doesn't have much to say about himself, other people can't seem to say enough about "Peter The Great."

STATS
Peter Forsberg

- Philadelphia's 1st pick (6th overall) 1991 NHL Entry Draft
- First NHL Team & Season — Quebec Nordiques 1994–95
- Born — July 20, 1973, in Ornskoldsvik, Sweden
- Position — Center
- Shoots — Left
- Height — 1.83 m (6')
- Weight — 85.5 kg (190 lbs.)

PETER FORSBERG

Center
COLORADO AVALANCHE

WAYNE GRETZKY
New York Rangers

Here is yet one more amazing fact about Wayne Gretzky: even if you don't count a single one of his 885 career goals, he would still be the all-time NHL points leader! Prior to the start of this season, Wayne had 1910 career assists. The next highest all-time points leader is Gordie Howe, who had 1850 total points (goals plus assists).

Wayne is the greatest playmaker in the history of the game. His ability to see the entire ice surface, to know where players are and where they are going to be, allows him to get the puck to his teammates while they are in a position to score. Wayne's great skill is that he puts the puck where his teammate is going to be, rather than where he is at the moment the pass is released.

"The game is so tight now in terms of checking," says Wayne. "It's very tough to find the open man . . . it's up to the player who is being covered to find the open ice. That's what I try to do with my passing now even more than I used to."

Wayne's signature play is where he sets up behind the opponent's net and passes the puck out to a teammate who is in scoring position in front of the net. Wayne estimates that 40 percent of his assists have come about as a result of this play.

"A coach I had in Junior B hockey told me to take the puck to the back of the net and try to set things up from there," recalls Wayne. "I really started to refine it and practice it then. It's sort of become my second home. Also, I'm not the biggest guy in the world and I found that the net offered me some protection and a little extra time to try to make something happen."

The things that Wayne can make happen often take even his teammates by surprise.

"One of the biggest things to get used to when playing with Wayne is that you always have to be ready for a pass no matter what the situation is," says former teammate and linemate Jari Kurri. "You may think that he's in a bad position . . . Then all of a sudden the puck will be there, right on your stick."

Philadelphia GM Bob Clarke says, "I think that people are going to look back and realize just how lucky they have been to watch Wayne Gretzky play hockey." Clarke continues: "I would have to say that he's the finest athlete Canada has ever produced. He's played more than 100 games every year for most of his life and produced like no one ever has."

STATS
Wayne Gretzky

- Reclaimed by Edmonton prior to Expansion Draft June, 1979
- First NHL Team & Season — Edmonton Oilers 1979–80
- Born — January 26, 1961 in Brantford, Ontario
- Position — Center
- Shoots — Left
- Height — 1.83 m (6')
- Weight — 81 kg (180 lbs.)

WAYNE GRETZKY

Center
NEW YORK RANGERS

JAROMIR JAGR
Pittsburgh Penguins

The Pittsburgh Penguins are now into their second season without the great Mario Lemieux to lead the team. And this season, like last, they are looking to Jaromir "Mario Jr." Jagr to provide the offensive fireworks that Pittsburgh hockey fans have come to expect. Jaromir didn't let the fans down last season: he led the NHL in scoring with 35 goals and 67 assists, for 102 points. Jaromir was the only player in the NHL last season to exceed 100 points. He also continued to cement his reputation as the best one-on-one player in the league. As one coach put it: "The best defence against Jagr is to hope that he's going to have an off night."

Philadelphia goalie Garth Snow says, "The biggest thing with Jagr is that he is so strong on the puck. You'll think someone is about to knock the puck off his stick and then all of sudden he's right in front of you and still with it . . . As a goalie, you always have to be aware of him."

As much as people talk about Jaromir replacing Mario Lemieux, Jaromir would be the first to tell you that he can't replace his former teammate, that he plays a different game than Mario did.

"Mario was like a quarterback. He liked to play with other guys and control things," says Jaromir. "I like to play more along the boards and one-on-one. I don't like people to say that it is my team. I can't do the same type of job that Mario did or that Wayne Gretzky does."

What Jaromir has done so far is very impressive. In eight NHL seasons he has averaged just over 37 goals per season. His best season so far was in 1995–96 when he scored 62 goals for Pittsburgh and assisted on 87 others for 149 points, a team record for a right winger. Jaromir won the league scoring title in the lockout-shortened 1994–95 season with 70 points in 48 games. He was also part of Pittsburgh's Stanley Cup Championship teams in 1991 and 1992. Not surprisingly, it is the Stanley Cup games that stand out in Jaromir's mind above all of the individual accomplishments.

"That was the best, the two Cups," says Jagr. "Playing with Mario, watching and learning from him . . . learning how to win. I was very lucky to learn from the best. You'll never find another player like him."

That may be true, but the Penguins are banking on Jaromir giving it his best shot.

STATS
Jaromir Jagr

- Pittsburgh's 1st pick (5th overall) 1990 NHL Entry Draft
- First NHL Team & Season — Pittsburgh Penguins 1990–91
- Born — February 15, 1972, in Kladno, Czechoslovakia
- Position — Right Wing
- Shoots — Left
- Height — 1.88 m (6'2")
- Weight — 97 kg (216 lbs.)

JAROMIR JAGR

Right Wing
PITTSBURGH PENGUINS

PAUL KARIYA
Mighty Ducks of Anaheim

There are several words to describe last season for Anaheim superstar Paul Kariya — nightmarish and frustrating are two that spring to mind. The descriptions have nothing to do with Paul's on-ice performance, mainly because there wasn't much of one. Unfortunately for Paul and hockey fans alike, last season seemed to go from one tough situation to another. Paul started the year locked in a contract battle with the Mighty Ducks. That dispute was resolved in early December and Paul returned to the Ducks' lineup. It was hoped that he would resume his leadership role with Anaheim and also play a big role with Canada's team at the Olympics. Paul had played with Canada at the 1994 Olympics and led the silver medal-winning team in scoring.

"I had been looking forward to returning to the Olympics for four years," said Paul at the time. "Playing in the Olympics is one of the greatest thrills a player can have and I really thought we had a great chance to win it this time around." (Canada ended up finishing fourth in Nagano.)

Paul's Olympic dream never materialized. He was cross-checked in the jaw by Chicago defenceman Gary Suter a couple of weeks before the Games. The cross-check caused a concussion that put Paul out of the Anaheim lineup for the rest of the season, and out of Canada's Olympic plans. Paul called having to back out of the Olympics the worst day of his life.

"I'm greatly disappointed this injury is prohibiting me from playing in the Olympics," said Paul. "Representing my country is the greatest honor anyone could have. I just wish I was healthy enough to compete."

There was great concern over Paul's concussion because it was his fourth. During the first few weeks after the injury, Paul got a headache just reading a book! You can understand why Anaheim team doctors were very careful about putting Paul back into the lineup.

Unfortunately, injuries are a part of hockey. But so is perseverance and dedication. Paul is one of the most intelligent and hard working players in the game today and there is nothing stopping him from coming back this season and leading his team in scoring. Anaheim fans are counting on it.

STATS
Paul Kariya

- Anaheim's 1st pick (4th overall) 1993 NHL Entry Draft
- First NHL Team & Season — Mighty Ducks of Anaheim 1994–95
- Born — October 16, 1974, in Vancouver, British Columbia
- Position — Left wing
- Shoots — Left
- Height — 1.80 m (5'11")
- Weight — 79 kg (175 lbs.)

PAUL ★ KARIYA

Left Wing
MIGHTY DUCKS OF ANAHEIM

JOHN LECLAIR
Philadelphia Flyers

If ever a change of scenery worked magic for an NHL player's career, John LeClair would be that player. In 224 games with the Montreal Canadiens, John accumulated 118 points. Since his trade to the Philadelphia Flyers in February of 1995, John has scored 330 points in 283 games, an average of 1.17 points per game.

"I guess I was in a bit of a rut in Montreal," recalls John. "I was getting mixed around on different lines, I wasn't getting ice time on the power play, that sort of thing. I really wasn't consistent and I wasn't playing much when I got traded . . . I think the trade was just something I needed at the time — a change of scenery."

Mark isn't the first player to have benefited from a trade to another organization. Another example is Buffalo goaltender Dominik Hasek. He wasn't able to crack the Chicago lineup for two seasons. The Blackhawks finally gave up on him and traded him to the Sabres in 1992. Two years later, Hasek won the Vezina Trophy and was named to the NHL's First All-Star Team.

"I think the Flyers organization allowed John's strengths to come to the surface," says assistant coach Wayne Cashman. "He's an incredible goal scorer, a natural who also works very hard at his game. He knows what his strengths are and uses them."

It also hasn't hurt that John has spent much of his career in Philadelphia playing on the same line as Eric Lindros.

"It helps your confidence to play on a line with a great player like Eric," says John. "When your confidence level is up, it helps you deal with the highs and lows — things come natural. But when the confidence isn't there you tend to press things a little more and that never helps."

Playing for the Flyers has been great for John. It is clear at this stage of his career that he could be a dominant player with any team. He has a very hard shot and drives to the net off the wing better than most players. He also has the toughness to play in front of the other team's net and take the ensuing punishment.

"The biggest thing for me in Philadelphia is that the team is winning and there is a tradition of winning," says John. "That's been the biggest similarity for me between the two teams [Montreal and Philadelphia]. The fans and management expect a winner and that makes us all work harder to be our best."

STATS
John LeClair

- Montreal's 2nd pick (33rd overall) 1987 NHL Entry Draft
- First NHL Team & Season — Montreal Canadiens 1990–91
- Born — July 5, 1969, in St. Albans, Vermont
- Position — Left Wing
- Shoots — Left
- Height — 1.90 m (6'3")
- Weight — 102 kg (226 lbs.)

John LeClair

Left Wing
PHILADELPHIA FLYERS

NICKLAS LIDSTROM
Detroit Red Wings

He may not have the explosive shot of Al MacInnis or the flash of Paul Coffey in his prime, but 28-year-old Nicklas Lidstrom is one of the most consistent and highly regarded defencemen in the NHL today.

"He's the first guy we think of to play in any situation," says Detroit associate coach Dave Lewis. "He plays both sides, he kills penalties, he's on the ice at the end of a game and he plays the power play. There's no time when he doesn't play. He's easily one of the top five or six defencemen in the NHL."

Check out the Detroit Red Wings in action and you'll see Nicklas on the ice against the other team's best players — one of the things to watch for to get an idea which defencemen the coach has the most confidence in.

"That's usually how we like to use Nicklas," says coach Scotty Bowman. "We like to have him out there against the other team's top offensive line. His main job is to prevent goals, not to score them. He's very underrated defensively."

Nicklas led all defencemen in scoring last season with 17 goals and 59 points. It was the third season in a row that Nicklas had scored 15 goals or more and topped the 55-point mark.

"Nick really stepped his game up last season," says Detroit General Manager Ken Holland. "He's taken charge, he gets more ice time and he's a huge part of our team."

Nick started in the NHL as a 21-year-old in the 1991–92 season. He was named to the NHL's All-Rookie Team with a total of 60 points in his first season. Prior to making his

way to the NHL, Nicklas picked up experience in the Swedish Elite League with Vasteras. He also helped Team Sweden win a gold medal at the 1991 World Championship.

"I was glad that I waited a couple of years after I was drafted to come to the NHL," says Nicklas. "I was more confident. Playing at the World Championship in 1991 against NHL players also helped my confidence."

World Championships, the Olympics, the Stanley Cup — Nicklas has done quite a bit considering he's only played six seasons in the NHL.

"I've been very lucky," says Nicklas. "I'm fortunate to have been able to play on some great teams with some great players."

Many of Nick's teammates would say the same thing about playing alongside him.

STATS
Nicklas Lidstrom

- Detroit's 3rd pick (53rd overall) 1989 NHL Entry Draft
- First NHL Team & Season — Detroit Red Wings 1991–92
- Born — April 28, 1970, in Vasteras, Sweden
- Position — Defence
- Shoots — Left
- Height — 1.88 m (6'2")
- Weight — 83 kg (185 lbs.)

NICKLAS LIDSTROM

Defence
DETROIT RED WINGS

ERIC LINDROS
Philadelphia Flyers

The decision was made prior to the announcement of Canada's Olympic hockey team lineup last November: Eric Lindros would wear the *C* as captain of the team.

"He is one of the best players in hockey," said Philadelphia GM Bob Clarke, general manager of that Olympic team. "As far as I'm concerned he's passed Gretzky and Messier and the other older players. He's been to the Olympics before [in 1994], he's played in the Canada Cup and the World Juniors. He captained his team to the Stanley Cup final. It is his time."

Despite the fact that Canada did not medal at the Winter Olympics, Eric still feels it was a worthwhile experience.

"I was floored to be named captain of the team and being at the Olympics was a great experience," says Eric. "Anytime you skate out there to represent your country you feel honored. I'm just disappointed we couldn't bring home the gold — our job was to go over there and win."

There was a lot of pressure on the Canadian Olympic team to win, but for Eric, handling pressure is almost second nature. Having been tagged as a superstar since he was 15 years old, Eric has had to learn how to handle all of the high expectations that go with that label.

"People always ask about pressure," says Eric. "The greatest pressure for me is my own personal pressure. I'm probably harder on myself and expect more from myself than anyone else does."

Those high personal expectations have definitely helped to fuel Eric's ongoing improvement as a player. Eric is a better skater, a better shooter and a more creative offensive player than he was when he broke into the NHL in 1992.

"Part of Eric's improvement and development as a player is a result of him being in situations where he has to really push himself and bring things up to the next level," says Bob Clarke.

The Flyers showed some confidence in Eric early last season by rewarding him with a contract extension worth $16-million. The deal will keep Eric with the Flyers through the rest of this season.

"I'm happy to be wearing this jersey for another season," said Eric after the contract announcement. "I want to be here and I want to be a winner here."

The Flyers hope the winning continues for many more seasons.

STATS
Eric Lindros

- Quebec's 1st pick (1st overall) 1991 NHL Entry Draft
- First NHL Team & Season — Philadelphia Flyers 1992–93
- Born — February 28, 1973, in London, Ontario
- Position — Center
- Shoots — Right
- Height — 1.93 m (6'4')
- Weight — 106 kg (236 lbs.)

MIKE MODANO
Dallas Stars

Putting together a combination of tremendous skill and experience has helped Mike Modano establish himself as one of the best players in the NHL. Early in his career, Mike relied on pure skill and natural talent to put up strong offensive numbers. However, as good as his offensive game could be, Mike's work as a defensive player left much to be desired. It is experience that has taught him the importance of having a strong, solid two-way game.

"I've learned that the team does better if you're a well-rounded player," says Mike. "If you play to win at both ends of the ice, the rest will look after itself."

The message "work as hard at defence as offence" is sometimes a tough one for coaches to convey to players who have made it to the NHL as big goal-scorers but weak defensive players.

"I know that when I played junior hockey, that's what people cared about," recalls Mike. "The more you scored the better you were, as simple as that. When I started my NHL career, it was the same way. I was expected to score. Now I'm expected to score, but the checking part of my game is important too."

Dallas coach Ken Hitchcock now uses Mike as one of his top penalty-killers and defensive forwards.

"I think that even if Mike doesn't score as much as he might like, the points he does get are more important than they were before," says Hitchcock. "His goals are worth more because his improved defensive play means that he doesn't give

up as many goals as he used to."

But don't get the mistaken impression that Mike has forgotten how to score. He has led the team in goals and points for two of the last three seasons. Last season, despite missing 30 games because of his injuries, Mike finished second in team scoring with 21 goals, 38 assists and 59 points.

Mike seems to enjoy his role with the Dallas Stars. His skill is put to use not only in situations where the team needs a big goal, but also where the team needs to protect a lead. Mike is the man the Stars count on to kill a penalty or take an important face-off late in a close game. Mike has always had the skill to excel in those situations, but now he has the experience and maturity as a player to go with the skill. Skill and experience — always a great combination.

STATS
Mike Modano

- Minnesota's 1st pick (1st overall) 1988 NHL Entry Draft

- First NHL Team & Season — Minnesota North Stars 1989–90

- Born — June 7, 1970, in Livonia, Michigan

- Position — Center

- Shoots — Left

- Height — 1.90 m (6'3")

- Weight — 200 lbs. (90 kg)

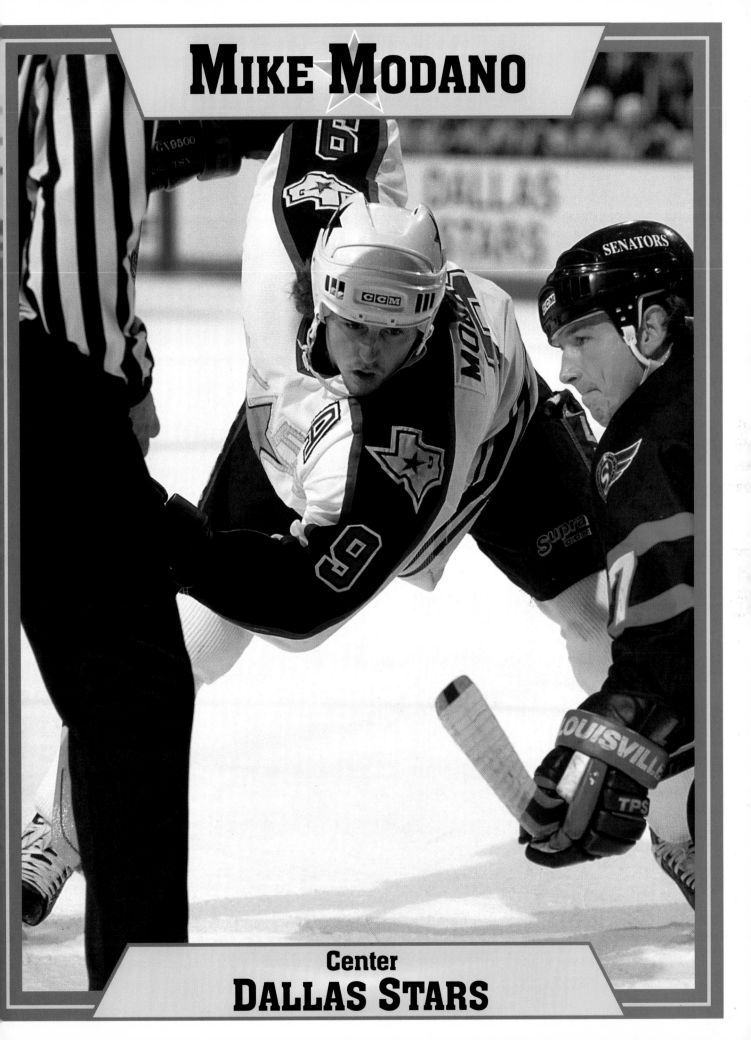

MIKE MODANO

Center
DALLAS STARS

MATTIAS OHLUND
Vancouver Canucks

One of the most difficult positions to learn in the NHL is defence. While it isn't unusual for a highly touted forward to step right into the NHL and earn a regular position on his new team, it is much more difficult for a defenceman to do so. There have been only a few exceptions. Brian Leetch stepped right in as a rookie defenceman with the New York Rangers back in 1988–89; and more recently, Brian Berard with the New York Islanders in 1996–97 and Vancouver's Mattias Ohlund last season.

"Mattias, without a doubt, is the best young defenceman I have ever coached," says Canucks bench boss Mike Keenan.

"As the year went on he showed that he was head and shoulders above any rookie in the league," says Colorado coach Mark Crawford. "There are guys who are good and are going to develop into decent players. But he is already a good player."

Mattias turns 22 this season and is heading into his second year in the NHL. Many other good young players start in the NHL as young as 19 years of age. But Mattias elected to remain in his native Sweden to play with his club team Lulea in the Swedish Elite League until everything was set for him to make the transition to the NHL.

"The extra year at home definitely helped me," says Mattias. "I gained confidence playing for Sweden at the 1997 World Championships. I got to test myself against the top Canadian and U.S. players. I saw that I was strong and fast enough to compete with these guys."

Mattias had a lot to contend with last season in Vancouver. On top of adjusting to life in the NHL and the highest caliber of play he had ever experienced, Mattias was also part of a team that sailed through some very rough water. The coach and general manager were both fired, there were numerous trades when new coach Mike Keenan came on board and there was also the increased pressure of having to play a big role on a defence that suffered numerous injuries.

"It has been a tough year, but a good year," said Mattias. "I got the chance to play with Pavel Bure and Mark Messier and against the best players in the world. It's always been my dream to play in the NHL."

No doubt that the next part of Mattias's dream involves wearing a few Stanley Cup rings before he calls it a career. And if last season is any indication, it will be a long and productive one.

STATS
Mattias Ohlund

- Vancouver's 1st pick (13th overall) 1994 NHL Entry Draft

- First NHL Team & Season — Vancouver Canucks 1997–98

- Born — September 9, 1976, in Pitea, Sweden

- Position — Defence

- Shoots — Left

- Height — 1.90 m (6'3")

- Weight — 94.1 kg (209 lbs.)

MATTIAS OHLUND

Defence
VANCOUVER CANUCKS

PATRICK ROY
Colorado Avalanche

Patrick Roy is a big-game goalie. In a pressure situation or a must-win game, Patrick has established himself time and time again as a goalie who will deliver.

"That's what great goaltending is all about," says his coach, Mark Crawford. "It comes up big at crucial times in games, and he's a master at that. He's going to win a lot more games. If he wants to he could probably play well into the next century. If he does that, he's going to get some records that are going to be pretty tough to beat."

Patrick already holds the NHL playoff records for most career wins and most games played. He is also the leader among active goaltenders with 41 career shut-outs and 380 career wins. Mix all of that with three Stanley Cup Championships and you have the recipe for a goaltender who can intimidate opponents just by showing up.

"Patrick is a goaltender you have to respect a great deal," says Wayne Gretzky. "I think one of the biggest challenges is to make sure you haven't psyched yourself out by thinking about how tough it is going to be to beat him."

"I have to have confidence in my game and what I can do. That is a big part of successful goaltending," says Patrick.

Patrick, like many goalies, is considered to be just a little different than other players on the team. Goalies have a reputation for being superstitious and sometimes, downright strange. It's what happens when you make your living having a frozen puck fired at you at speeds of over 130 kilometres per hour!

Patrick has been known to write his children's names on his goalie stick for good luck, to talk to himself during games and to crane his neck and shrug his shoulders during stoppages in play. The funny thing is that the more Patrick does these things, the better he seems to play.

"Yeah, Patrick has some odd mannerisms," smiles coach Crawford. "He does some of those things to make himself comfortable. The important thing to me is that he is comfortable and can go about his business the way he has to."

"I don't think about those things too much," says Patrick. "I do those things to help me to focus and concentrate."

Whatever it is Patrick does, he gets the job done — and that's the bottom line in the very competitive world of pro hockey.

STATS
Patrick Roy

- Montreal's 4th pick (51st overall) 1984 NHL Entry Draft
- First NHL Team & Season — Montreal Canadiens 1985–86
- Born — October 5, 1965, in Quebec City, Quebec
- Position — Goaltender
- Catches — Left
- Height — 1.83 m (6')
- Weight — 87 kg (192 lbs.)

PATRICK ROY

Goaltender
COLORADO AVALANCHE

MATS SUNDIN
Toronto Maple Leafs

Being a great player on a not-so-great team can be a tough grind. No matter how much individual success a player achieves, the ultimate prize is still to be part of a team that wins the Stanley Cup or, at the very least, has a solid chance to contend for the Cup.

For Toronto captain Mats Sundin, individual recognition has long since arrived. He was the first overall pick in the NHL Entry Draft in 1989, he scored the gold-medal winning goal for Sweden at the 1991 World Hockey Championship and he was a dominant force for Team Sweden during the 1996 World Cup. However, a legitimate run at the Stanley Cup is something that Mats has yet to come close to during his eight-year NHL career. In eight seasons, he has only played in the Stanley Cup playoffs three times, and he has never played for a team that has advanced past the first round of the post-season.

While Mats was with the Quebec Nordiques, they were struggling their way up the NHL ranks. And since his trade to Toronto, Mats has been part of a Leafs team on a downward slide.

"We have some good young kids coming along, but we're definitely in a rebuilding stage here," says Mats. "The toughest part is not getting to the playoffs — that hurts bad."

Not making the playoffs not only hurts the Leafs, but it also hurts Mats's reputation as a bona fide superstar of the game. For Mats to take that next step and be mentioned in the same breath as players like Jaromir Jagr, Eric Lindros and Paul Kariya, he needs to lead the Leafs through a successful playoff run. It will be tough for Mats to do that until the team around him becomes more competitive.

A couple of seasons ago Toronto coach Mike Murphy called it when he said, "For Mats to take the next step and become a player mentioned with Lindros and those guys, the team has to get better. He needs the team to push him upwards rather than having to be carried by him."

Prior to the start of last season, Mats was named the 16th captain in the history of the Toronto Maple Leafs. The honor has put even more pressure on him to succeed.

"I know people expect more from me," says Mats, "but I expect more too. I know that I've really started to come into my own as a hockey player in the last couple of years. But I also know that doing it in the playoffs is what really counts and that's what I want to do."

STATS
Mats Sundin

- Quebec's 1st pick (1st overall) 1989 NHL Entry Draft
- First NHL Team & Season — Quebec Nordiques 1990–91
- Born — February 13, 1971, Bromma, Sweden
- Position — Center/Right Wing
- Shoots — Right
- Height — 1.93 m (6'4")
- Weight — 97 kg (215 lbs.)

MATS SUNDIN

Center/Right Wing
TORONTO MAPLE LEAFS

KEITH TKACHUK
PHOENIX COYOTES

Keith Tkachuk is everything you want a great hockey player to be: talented, aggressive, and a little cocky. Part of what makes him as good as he is is a large dash of self-confidence. It would be very difficult, if not impossible, to make your living in the NHL if you didn't believe in yourself and your ability. Ask almost any pro athlete about the role confidence plays, and the answer is almost always: "A huge part, I couldn't succeed without it."

Keith is one of the best goal scorers in the NHL today. He is a power forward who is at his best when he's driving towards the net to get a shot away or cash in on a rebound. He has topped the 50-goal mark two of the last three seasons. He led his team in scoring last season with 40 goals and 66 points.

"I've never really thought of myself as a goal-scorer," says Keith. "I just try to keep things basic and simple, go to the net and pay the price and sacrifice my body. I can't play well unless I'm getting my nose dirty."

Keith certainly takes his share of penalties. He has topped 200 penalty minutes in a season three times.

"Those are penalties that are a result of hard work and trying to make things happen, penalties for not backing down in certain situations," says coach Jim Schoenfeld.

Coyotes General Manager Bobby Smith feels that the skill aspect of Keith's game gets overlooked because of the tough physical game that he plays.

"He has more skill than I ever imagined," says Smith. "People tend to think of his goals as Keith hammering someone or driving one home from two feet out in a scramble. But I've seen him score from all over. I've seen him score some pretty goals and make great plays. He has a great pair of hands."

Those who know Keith will tell you that he has matured a great deal in the last couple of seasons. He's 26 years old and, while he hasn't exactly mellowed, he is much more controlled both on and off the ice.

"People sometimes misunderstand Keith. He's confident and has an ego just like any pro athlete," says Bobby Smith. "But he doesn't have to be the man. He just wants to win. Winning the Cup means everything to him. That's what drives him."

And with Keith driving hard towards that goal, you get the feeling the rest of the Coyotes will be driving just as hard.

STATS
Keith Tkachuk

- Winnipeg's 1st pick (19th overall) 1990 NHL Entry Draft
- First NHL Team & Season — Winnipeg Jets 1991–92
- Born — March 28, 1972, in Melrose, Massachusetts
- Position — Left wing
- Shoots — Left
- Height — 1.88 m (6'2")
- Weight — 90 kg (200 lbs.)

Keith Tkachuk

Left Wing
Phoenix Coyotes

ALEXI YASHIN
Ottawa Senators

Alexi Yashin is easily one of the top 10 centermen in the NHL. Unfortunately, the team he plays for hasn't cracked the top 10 yet — but with hard work, good coaching and some talented players, they will get there. Consider that just two seasons ago the Senators finished with only 18 wins and an abysmal 291 goals scored against them. Since then, point totals have gone up and goals-given-up totals have gone down.

The Senators are blessed with a cast of very promising young players. Defencemen Wade Redden and Chris Phillips anchor a maturing blue line. And, up front, they are led by the likes of Daniel Alfredsson and Alexi Yashin.

"We really want to take this team to the next level," says Alexi. "To do that we all have to be ready every night. We've taken some good steps and the people in Ottawa are excited about the team, but we have to work even harder than we have in the past."

Part of being on a successful team means being unselfish. Personal goals are important, but in the NHL they have to take a back seat to team goals. Alexi has been accused in the past of not buying into the "team first" concept; some people claimed Alexi was selfish and aloof. However, those who know him well tell of a different side to Alexi. That side was very evident last season when Alexi made a donation of $1-million to the National Arts Centre in Ottawa.

"We do make a lot of money," says Alexi, "and I think that it's great when you can give something back to the community, especially to kids who may now get a chance to see performing arts for free. It just seemed like the right thing to do. I enjoy the performing arts and I'm just glad I could help."

Alexi would like to see some of the money put to use to promote the culture of his native Russia in Canada by bringing some of Russia's great performers to Ottawa to perform. Tops on the list of people he'd like to see perform would be the world famous Russian ballet dancer Mikhail Baryshnikov. That would make it two great Russian stars performing in Ottawa!

STATS
Alexi Yashin

- Ottawa's 1st pick (2nd overall) 1992 NHL Entry Draft
- First NHL Team & Season — Ottawa Senators 1993–94
- Born — November 5, 1973, in Sverdlovsk, USSR
- Position — Center
- Shoots — Right
- Height — 1.90 m (6'3")
- Weight — 97 kg (215 lbs.)

ALEXI YASHIN

Center
OTTAWA SENATORS

Do You Know. . . ?

1. What current NHL head coach never missed the playoffs during his 20-year playing career?

2. What is the highest number of goals scored by one player in an NHL playoff game?

3. Who has won more games than any other American-born NHL goaltender?

4. For how many teams has Philadelphia coach Roger Neilson served as head coach?

5. What are the highest and lowest point totals ever recorded by an NHL team in a minimum 80-game schedule?

6. What NHL player took more shots on goal than any other last season? How many goals did he score?

7. Who was the first non-North American player to be taken first overall in the NHL Entry Draft?

8. Name the multiple winners of the Calder Memorial Trophy.

8. There are no multiple winners! A player can only win the award in his first (rookie) season in the NHL.

7. Mats Sundin, born in Bromma, Sweden, was drafted first overall by the Quebec Nordiques in 1989.

6. Pavel Bure of the Vancouver Canucks took 329 shots on goal in 82 games. He ended up with 51 goals, 39 assists and 90 points.

5. The Montreal Canadiens recorded 132 points in the 1976–77 season. The Washington Capitals recorded 21 points in 1974–75.

4. Roger Neilson has been the head coach of eight NHL teams.

3. Pittsburgh's Tom Barasso has won more games than any other American-born NHL goalie.

2. Frank McGee, of the Ottawa Silver Seven, scored 14 goals in a single game on January 16, 1905. Ottawa defeated Dawson City 23-2!

1. Los Angeles head coach Larry Robinson.

The All-Star Game
About halfway through the season there is an All-Star game played in one NHL city. The game features the All-Stars from the Western Conference against the All-Stars from the Eastern Conference.
   Fill this in right after you watch the game on television.

Date of game: _____   Where was it played? _____

Winning team: _____

Final score: _____

The winning goal was scored by: _____

Most valuable player of the game (MVP): _____

Highlights of the Game
The following players scored:

_____   _____

_____   _____

_____   _____

_____   _____

The best play of the game was when: _____

_____

The best save was when: _____

_____

Other highlights: _____

_____

_____

_____

_____

Penalties

Do you know what is happening when the referee stops play and makes a penalty call? If you don't, then you're missing an important part of the game. The referee can call different penalties that result in everything from playing a man short for two minutes to having a player kicked out of the game.

Here are some of the most common referee signals. Now you'll know what penalties are being called against your team.

Boarding
Pounding the closed fist of one hand into the open palm of the other hand.

Charging
Rotating clenched fists around one another in front of the chest.

Cross-checking
A forward and backward motion with both fists clenched extending from the chest.

Elbowing
Tapping the elbow of the "whistle hand" with the opposite hand.

High-sticking
Holding both fists, clenched, one above the other.

Holding
Clasping the wrist of the "whistle hand" well in front of the chest.

Hooking
A tugging motion with both arms, as if pulling something toward the stomach.

Roughing
A thrusting motion with the arm extending from the side.

Interference
Crossed arms stationary in front of the chest with fists closed.

Slashing
A chopping motion with the edge of one hand across the opposite forearm.

Tripping
Striking the right leg with the right hand below the knee while keeping both skates on the ice.

Wash-out
Both arms swung laterally across the body with palms facing down. Used by the referee, it means no goal.

Spearing
A jabbing motion with both hands thrust out in front of the body.

Unsportsmanlike conduct
Use both hands to form a "T" in front of the chest.

Your Own Hockey Career

Whether you play in a league, at school, or just for recreation, it's fun to keep track of how you and your team do during the season.

This section is for you to fill in with the details of your hockey career — both the high points and the low points.

Your team's name: _____

Name of the league: _____

Position you play: _____

Your team nickname: _____

Some of the other players on the team:

_____   _____

_____   _____

_____   _____

_____   _____

_____   _____

_____   _____

_____   _____

_____   _____

Season Highlights
The most exciting game you played in this season was: _____

_____

_____

Your own best game was: _____

_____

_____

_____

★ ★ ★ YOUR RECORD KEEPER ★ ★ ★

The best team you played against this season was: _____

_____

The closest game you played was: _____

_____

Your worst game was: _____

_____

_____

The funniest thing that happened to you during a hockey game this season was:

_____

_____

Here's your own personal score sheet — fill this out after every game.

	OTHER TEAM	GOALS	ASSISTS	POINTS
GAME #1				
GAME #2				
GAME #3				
GAME #4				
GAME #5				
GAME #6				
GAME #7				
GAME #8				
GAME #9				
GAME #10				

The Stanley Cup Playoffs

The Stanley Cup Playoffs start in April and usually run until the end of May. Before reaching the final, teams must first win their respective Division and Conference championships.

Keep track below:

Pacific Division Champion: _____

Central Division Champion: _____

Western Conference Champion: _____

Atlantic Division Champion: _____

Northeast Division Champion: _____

Eastern Division Champion: _____

Stanley Cup Final

Which two teams played? _____

Who won? _____

How many games did the series go to? _____

Who was the Playoff MVP? _____

Clip a picture from the newspaper of the winning team
with the Stanley Cup after the final game. Tape the picture below.

The Final — Game-by-Game

Fill out this part of your record keeper after each game of the
Stanley Cup Final while you can still feel the excitement!
Fill in the final score, where the game was played, who scored
and any other information you can think of.

```
GAME
1    _____
     _____
     _____

GAME
2    _____
     _____
     _____

GAME
3    _____
     _____
     _____

GAME
4    _____
     _____
     _____

GAME
5    _____
     _____
     _____

GAME
6    _____
     _____
     _____

GAME
7    _____
     _____
     _____
```

NHL Awards

Here are some of the major NHL awards for individual players. Fill in your selection for each award and then fill in the name of the actual winner of the trophy.

HART MEMORIAL TROPHY

Awarded to the player judged to be the most valuable to his team. Selected by the Professional Hockey Writers Association.

Your choice: _____   The winner: _____

ART ROSS TROPHY

Awarded to the player who leads the league in scoring points at the end of the regular season.

Your choice: _____   The winner: _____

CALDER MEMORIAL TROPHY

Awarded to the player selected as the most proficient in his first year of competition in the NHL. Selected by the Professional Hockey Writers Association.

Your choice: _____   The winner: _____

JAMES NORRIS TROPHY

Awarded to the defence player who demonstrates throughout his season the greatest all-round ability. Selected by the Professional Hockey Writers Association.

Your choice: _____   The winner: _____

VEZINA TROPHY

Awarded to the goalkeeper judged to be the best. Selected by the NHL general managers.

Your choice: _____   The winner: _____

14506